CAPITAL
of
HEAVEN

Marc Riboud

CAPITAL
of
HEAVEN

Introduction François Cheng

Doubleday
New York · London · Toronto · Sydney · Auckland

I WOULD LIKE TO THANK JACQUELINE KENNEDY ONASSIS,
WHO WAS THE FIRST TO BELIEVE THAT THOSE MISTY SNAPSHOTS COULD MAKE A BOOK.
— M.R.

PUBLISHED BY DOUBLEDAY
A DIVISION OF BANTAM DOUBLEDAY DELL PUBLISHING GROUP, INC.
666 FIFTH AVENUE, NEW YORK, NEW YORK 10103

DOUBLEDAY AND THE PORTRAYAL OF AN ANCHOR
WITH A DOLPHIN ARE TRADEMARKS OF DOUBLEDAY,
A DIVISION OF BANTAM DOUBLEDAY DELL
PUBLISHING GROUP, INC.

LIBRARY OF CONGRESS CATALOGING-IN-PUBLICATION DATA
RIBOUD, MARC.
CAPITAL OF HEAVEN BY MARC RIBOUD: INTRODUCTION BY FRANÇOIS CHENG —
1ST ED. IN THE UNITED STATES OF AMERICA
P. CM.
1. HUANG MOUNTAINS (CHINA) — DESCRIPTION AND TRAVEL — VIEWS
I. TITLE
DS793.H669R53 1990
915.1'225 — DC20   89-48673, CIP

ISBN 0-385-19665-2
COPYRIGHT © 1990 BY MARC RIBOUD
TRANSLATION COPYRIGHT © 1990 BY DOUBLEDAY,
A DIVISION OF BANTAM DOUBLEDAY DELL PUBLISHING GROUP, INC.

TRANSLATED BY JESSIE WOOD
DESIGN BY PHILIP HARTLEY

PHOTOCOMPOSITION, PHOTOENGRAVING, AND OFFSET-LITHO PRINTING
BY JEAN GENOUD SA, LAUSANNE, SWITZERLAND
ALL RIGHTS RESERVED
PRINTED IN SWITZERLAND
NOVEMBER 1990
FIRST EDITION IN THE UNITED STATES OF AMERICA

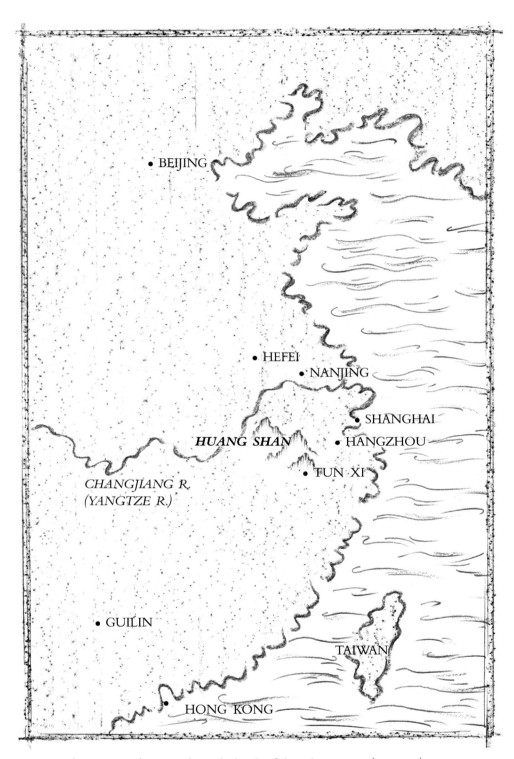

The Huang Shan, on the right bank of the Changjiang (Yangtze) River,

is the mountain of painters and poets.

BROKEN LAND—

MOUNTAINS, RIVERS ENDURE

TU FU, EIGHTH CENTURY

Pines and cliffs on Mount Huang by Hongren,

seventeenth century.

■

OF ALL THE MOUNTAINS OF CHINA, LET US HONOR THE HUANG SHAN.
Noblest of them all, this range lies in the heart of China. Through the splendor of its sites, which together
form a whole full of both contrast and harmony; through the strange dialogue between pines and rocks,
with their everlasting and fantastic air, a dialogue punctuated by the echoes of springs and waterfalls;
through the presence of mists and clouds, fascinating for the nuanced coloring and ever-changing motion
which crowns them with a mystery ceaselessly renewed; and, finally, through all the myths that cling to
this sacred place frequented by figures of legend and by the greatest painters and poets down through the
centuries, the Huang Shan embodies to perfection all that is deepest and most constant in the Chinese
imagination.

What does the mountain represent, in Chinese eyes? The answer lies in Chinese cosmology, in
which the primordial breath of life, emanating from the original chaos, is divided into two vital forces,
Yang and Yin, whose continual interplay governs the workings of the ten thousand beings of the created
world. The Yang and the Yin, respectively representing active force and passive receptivity, are present at
various levels of the living universe in coupled entities. Thus the Sky-Yang forms a couple with the
Earth-Yin, the Sun-Yang with the Moon-Yin, the Mountain-Yang with the Water-Yin, and so forth.
Yet there is nothing rigid or static in these relationships. Thanks to the Median Void, which governs their
interaction, the two entities in the couple are in a state of tensile attraction, forming a harmonious whole.
They respond to each other. Each, while endowed with its own property, Yang or Yin, seeks out its part-
ner and thus assumes the other's qualities. Ideally, therefore, the true Yang must contain Yin, and Yin
must contain Yang. Just as in the human couple, where man has some feminine traits and woman some
masculine ones, the mountain is not imprisoned in its Yang nature. Recalling its origin as "an arrested
wave," it constantly seeks to assume the characteristics of water. As for water, though Yin in nature, does
it not show Yang when it rises up as a mighty wave? Thus Nature, despite its apparent rigor, reveals itself
as a dynamic whole, in perpetual flux. Let us emphasize that the mountain, compared to other entities, is
exceptional in being complete in itself. Primarily Yang because of its crags and peaks, it does not lack for
Yin, thanks to its springs and waterfalls. Above all, the mountain harbors in its breast mists and clouds
that lure it into secret internal metamorphoses. In the Chinese imagination, the cloud, a condensation of

water with the shape of a mountain, is a perfect example of the Median Void, a manifestation of the two natures. With its flanks shrouded by mist and cloud, the mountain seems ready to fall and melt into water, while water appears equally likely to rear itself up and become a mountain. Thus the mountain embodies within itself a circular movement that is both basic and exemplary.

Now we can better understand why Chinese sages and artists have sought so ardently to commune with the mountain. They happily lose themselves among the "thousand peaks and ten thousand grottoes," to admire certain beautiful sites, of course, but above all to renew themselves at the source of the vital forces which give life to the universe, reestablish the links between heaven and earth, and—according to the Taoist dream—confer immortality. It is hardly astonishing that the ideogram for the word "immortal" is composed of the sign for "man" and the sign for "mountain," and that the entire word stands for a millennial and authentic wisdom.

In the eighth century, Li Po (whose presence in the Huang Shan gave rise to a beautiful legend of which we will speak later), the great poet of the Tang dynasty, ever in search of hermits and of total communion with Creation, made frequent sojourns in the mountains. There is not a notable peak in China unmarked by his passage. He described his rich experiences in the famous quatrain entitled "To My Friend Who Questions Me":

Why stay in the bosom of these green mountains?

I smile, serene at heart.

Peach blossom, at the mercy of water: mysterious way...

Another heaven-earth, not that of men!

Through the ages, Chinese artists painting the mountain have inevitably re-created a fluid space where finite meets infinite.

In this cosmological and artistic tradition the Huang Shan enjoys a privileged place, even though other mountains, such as the Five Sacred Peaks, situated at the cardinal points of China, are held in high esteem. Rising in the heart of the vast Middle Kingdom, the Huang Shan represents the point of equilibrium where north meets south, and where the river Changjiang (Yangtze), flowing from west to east, feeding a constellation of lakes, adds to the splendor of the landscape.

Furthermore, the typical scenery of the Huang Shan, bathed in ever-changing pastel mists, represents the ideal of Chinese painting. When exclaiming over a beautiful picture, one is apt to say that it is "truer than nature." At the foot of the Huang Shan, the awed spectator invariably exclaims, "It's truer than Chinese painting!" Granted that these paintings are often landscapes so ethereal, so unreal that they seem to have been invented by the artists. Yet the Huang Shan is one of the places in China which invalidates this impression. Painters have always been inspired by the Huang Shan, but it was with the beginning of the seventeenth century and the fall of the Ming dynasty that it became an integral part of Chinese pictorial art. A group of eminent painters—Hongren, Mei Qing, Shitao, Kuncan, and others—came here for long stays and formed a school of painting. Ever since, the Huang Shan has been a veritable cradle of art. Every new school has come here to seek energy and inspiration. To mention a few greats of the modern age, Huang Binhong, Zhang Daqian, Fu Baoshi all conceived a passion for these mountains. Today, after the terrible years of the Cultural Revolution, painters have once again returned to the Huang Shan to find inspiration for the renewal of the great tradition of the past. An urgent, touching need has led hundreds—perhaps thousands—of them to make the pilgrimage to the Huang Shan, to come and to return again and again. They are now part of the scenery.

The Huang Shan is in the central province of Anhui, south of the Changjiang River. The chain includes a great number of peaks, seventy-two of which, according to tradition, are considered famous. In the heart of this impressive massif rise about twenty high peaks with steep, jagged cliffs and deep ravines. The three highest summits, all under 6,100 feet, are the Capital of Heaven to the south, the Lotus Blossom to the west, and farther north, the Luminous Peak. Two other important peaks join the triangle formed by these three mountains: the Jade Screen, located between the Capital of Heaven and the Lotus Blossom, and the Snow Goose, in the North Sea area. The five principal mountains are connected by footpaths which offer the tourist vertiginous views of the very heart of the Huang Shan. Long a restricted paradise, open only to collectors of rare medicinal plants and to ardent mountaineers with time and money to spare, the Huang Shan is now easily accessible. The visitor enters the Huang Shan by the South Gate, marked by a huge archway. Following the motor road, he soon reaches the Hot Springs area, at an altitude of 2,060 feet. Here there are several hotels. These are the oldest tourist accommodations in the Huang Shan. Enjoyment of the thermal baths is enhanced by the exotic scenery on every side. On arriving in this part of the Huang Shan, the visitor immediately notices the air, redolent of greenery and flowers, cheerful with the burble of the springs. The River of the Peach Trees meanders through the valley, watched over by the Hill of the Crimson Clouds and the Hill of the Peach Blossoms.

Close to the hotel and to one's right is the Pavilion of Contemplation, from which one can admire the Thousand Fathom Falls and the Nine Dragons Cascade. To the left, the observation tower offers a splendid view of the Sign of Man Waterfall, also called, for the benefit of Westerners, the Waterfall of the Inverted V. As the visitor continues along the riverbank, a strange music, crystalline in tone, will suddenly strike his ear. This is the voice of the Cascade of the Strummed Zither. The falling water strikes a rock lying slightly aslant, creating an ever-varying melody. This music from time immemorial carries the visitor back to the eighth century and invites him to remember the great poet Li Po. Legend has it that when Li Po came to the Huang Shan and first heard this waterfall, he fell under its spell. He sat down on a nearby boulder and, soothed by the music, drank wine and composed a verse cycle. Drunkenly, he stretched out on the rock, knocking over his goblet of wine. The wine impregnated the stone, which in turn became drunk. To commemorate this event sometime later, the words "Drunken Rock" were carved on the side of the boulder.

As the visitor makes his way back toward the Hot Springs, he will admire at every rise in the path the magnificent views. In the distance, far above the tree line, rise the high granite peaks with their contrasting colors and shapes: the Capital of Heaven, the Lotus Blossom, and between them the Jade Screen. From here the visitor has two choices: to go west toward the Jade Screen, on which a pavilion of the same name has been built, or to go east to the Temple of the Vale of Clouds, point of departure for an aerial cable car to the peak of the Snow Goose, on which stands the North Sea Hotel. The Hot Springs area, the Jade Screen area, and the North Sea area all offer accommodations. Any of the three can serve as a base from which the tourist may explore—and perhaps even penetrate for a moment—the secret of the Huang Shan.

Nestled in a hollow at the peak, at an altitude of 5,400 feet, the Jade Screen Hotel is a converted temple, which long ago offered shelter to many guests, illustrious or obscure. The flanks of the mountain on which it stands are composed of smooth stone slabs, set one against the other vertically, like a harmonious arrangement of petals of jade. It greatly resembles an ancient Chinese screen, with bright scenes in mosaics of jade and mica. Looking at the mountain in a slight haze, one can almost see figures rising up and going on their way to a place beyond time.

Behind the hotel and close by is a small tarn, one of three or four scattered on the heights of the Huang Shan. As in a limpid mirror, the delicate colors change with every capricious movement of the clouds above and of the tremulous shadows of the surrounding pines. Here the visitor is struck by the rustling and the fragrance of the famous Huang Shan pines, whose tortuous and enigmatic silhouettes are etched against the sky. Some are twisted into shapes that suggest great lords making ritual gestures: Pine-Welcoming-the-Guests, Pine-Bidding-Farewell, Pine-Prayer-Cushion....

Also most imposing are the fantastically shaped granite rocks, whose names are fully as evocative: Rock-of-the-Squirrel-Leaping-Toward-the-Capital-of-Heaven, Rock-of-the-Three-Immortal-Isles, Rock-of-the-Peacock-Playing-with-a-Lotus.... Continuing a little farther, the visitor will see the justly famous Rock-Come-from-Elsewhere-Flying. On the smooth brink of a precipice, there stands, rather precariously, a vertical slab 40 feet high, weighing 360 tons, leaning like the Tower of Pisa. A relic of the Ice Age, like all the other rocks, it was deposited here in an "eternally momentary" pose, like some giant bird alighting for an instant before taking to the air once more.

We must now mention a certain fact of striking significance: here in the Huang Shan, pines and rocks are intimately involved with each other. It is not a matter of solidarity but of inseparability. Many of the pines are actually rooted in rock, from which they have struggled forth by brute force. Their roots secrete an acid which erodes the rock, transforming it into a sort of humus. In spite of wind and storm, the pines persevere. Pines and rocks seem lost in a contrapuntal game, of which they never tire, so varied are the poses they strike, so contrasted their relationship. Some of the rocks are a soft mauve, others a shining black. Austere boulders gravely stand at attention, while other rocks seem soft and rounded, like a woman's breasts. Entwined amidst them, the pines, silver or emerald, some reaching for the sky with outstretched arms, others gnarled and bent, play with shadows. What especially touches the Chinese soul—beyond the elegant rites celebrated by the vegetable and mineral kingdoms—is the profound *dialogue, full of connivance, carried on between the two of them, one clinging tenaciously to the soil, the other straining to touch the heavens: a contrast of grace and rigor, profoundly moving to the human spirit. Here is the circular movement of reciprocity mentioned in our discussion of Chinese cosmology. A Taoist poem says:*

> *Rock thrusting forth tree*
>
> *Tree breathing in rock*
>
> *Open circle tightening bond of earth and sky*
>
> *Closed circle renewing three-faceted mystery*
>
> *Under the proffered shade wandering man*
>
> *At last finds his kingdom*

Besides its intrinsic beauty, the Jade Screen area offers the tourist a chance to visit the two most majestic mountains, Capital of Heaven and Lotus Blossom, which lie on either side of it. Before scaling their heights, the tourist may admire at his leisure these two splendid peaks, rearing up like the towers of an imaginary cathedral: the one, majestic, polished by time, shrouded in haughtiness; the other, flamboyant, draped in purple, sinuously furrowed, opening like a huge flower.

If the visitor has time for only one peak, he should not hesitate to choose the Capital of Heaven, by far the more breathtaking climb. From its foot, one can already see, cutting across the cliffs and rock faces, thousands of steps, some carved into the mountainside, others more like stepping-stones. These steps represent the hard and dangerous work of generations of men. Those who climb the stairway in Indian file may rightly feel that they have been passed the torch by those who went before them and that they are passing it on to those who are to follow. The most dangerous passage is across a long, narrow vertical face known as the Carp's Back. Only one person can cross at a time. No matter how he concentrates, the climber, clutching the rickety chains on either side of the steps, cannot help but glance at the vertiginous depths below him. This is truly a rite of passage, for it is here, shaken by the earth's vibrations in time with the cosmos, that he enters into sensual communion with the Huang Shan. On the top is his reward: a spectacular view of the entire Huang Shan range, a magnificent and deeply moving sight that assails the senses from every side. We shall not seek words to describe the experience. Let everyone dream of it—or someday live it! The climber may also enjoy the beauty of the scenery from the summits of the Lotus Blossom and the Luminous Peak, which, along with the Capital of Heaven, are the highest points in the Huang Shan.

The North Sea Hotel can be reached rapidly by cable car. Built on a plateau and surrounded by Snow Goose Peak, Luminous Peak, and Crouching Lion Mountain, this tourist center offers the visitor easy access to the many exceptional sites nearby. Probably the most famous of these is Mount Now-I-Believe-It. As the name suggests, this mountain, shaped like a promontory, is ideally located and offers a superb view of clusters of peaks, varied and striking in their form, stretching into the distance. Among them is Bamboo Shoot Mountain with its rows of gigantic stalagmites, a forest of granite bamboos, from the midst of which the Chinese believe that they can glimpse the Eighteen-Buddhas-Bowing-to-the-South-Sea. A little farther on is an area verdant with plants and flowers. In the middle stands a large vertical boulder crowned with a lone pine. This harmonious composition has inspired poets through the ages and bears the poetic name Flower-Formed-on-the-Tip-of-a-Dream-Paintbrush. Always in perfect symbiosis with the rocks, individual pines impose their presence: Black Tiger, Reclining Dragon, the Unicorn, the Inseparable Lovers.

Moving on, the traveler enters an immense forest of pines, whose rustle and sigh can be heard from afar. Here in the heart of still-unspoiled nature, one is again reminded that the Huang Shan is a rich preserve of rare plants and flowers, birds and animals. Plants such as the ginkgo, the actinidia, and tinder fungus are famous for their medicinal or aphrodisiac qualities. The presence of pheasants, deer, and monkeys adds to the exoticism of the scene. Among the myriads of birds, two are especially worth noting: the octave, a bird whose melodious voice has an astonishing range, and the migratory bird called sorrow-of-love, which comes here twice a year, in early spring and late autumn, for the Huang Shan lies athwart one of the great migration flyways of the world.

But the main attraction, the spectacle that most captivates visitors to the North Sea area, is the everlasting, ever-changing play of mists and clouds. "North Sea" refers to the sea of clouds. Here, as in the South Sea, the East Sea, and the West Sea, the cloudplay transforms the range into an archipelago of floating islands. In the Huang Shan, mist and cloud are in such osmosis with the mountain that the visitor has a hallucinatory impression of mountain being but one of their states, a momentarily stable one, or else that cloud and mist are mountain made fluid. Purple or azure, tinted or luminous, their palette harmonizes with that of the rocks and vegetation. They drift up from the valley to swirl around one peak, then another, luring the mountains into endless metamorphoses. As if performing a sacred rite, the visitor climbs at drawn to the high terrace of the Crouching Lion to see the fleeting clouds pierced by the rising sun, and at day's end he is inexorably drawn to the west, to the Belvedere-of-the-Unfurling-Clouds, to watch the cloud tide engulf the setting sun. At such hours, mountains, pines, rocks, the Monkey-Contemplating-the-Ocean, the Goddess-Offering-Flowers, the Immortal-Drying-His-Boots, all stand motionless, silhouetted in the foreground; all of nature seems spellbound. One can never tire of this grandiose spectacle, as light and illusion change from one second to the next.

Here again, words are inadequate to express the deep feelings the Chinese harbor for clouds and mist: evanescent and elusive, yet to their minds, almost fleshly in substance. Their relationship with them is close to sensual. Do not their poets speak of "sleeping in the bosom of mist and cloud," and of "caressing cloud and mist"? Disciples of Taoism counsel us to "feed upon mist and cloud." In the Huang Shan, clouds and mist keep us in constant suspense, as we await their coming, regret their going. When they appear, we allow ourselves to be enveloped in their silken and fleecy embrace, we breathe in their fragrance of sandalwood. When they go, we are dazed, bedazzled by the blinding visions they have left behind. This is more than simple distraction; it is true love.

By its multiplicity of peaks, formed into an organic whole, by its precious plants and its rare fauna, by the extraordinary colloquy between pine and rock, by the mystery imparted by mist and cloud, the Huang Shan exerts an irresistible fascination. It resonates deep in the heart of Chinese sensibility and imagination, so much so that the painter Zao Wou-ki advises his Western friends who wish to grasp the essence of the Chinese landscape: "If you have never been to the Huang Shan, you have no idea of what a Chinese landscape is!" In Chinese eyes, it is a primordial space, haunted by myth—the more so because many of its sites seem to embody the mythical themes that all Chinese carry in their souls. We have already seen that the names given to springs, pines, rocks, and other features evoke with eloquence the myths and legends that lie deep in the collective imagination. Even the name Huang Shan *is a primordial metaphor. It means "Yellow Mountain," the "yellow" being a reference to the Yellow Emperor (c. 2700 B.C.), first ancestor of the Chinese race, founder of China. According to legend, at the end of his long life, his work accomplished, he chose to live out his days in the Huang Shan. Accompanied by two loyal subjects, he went to the top of the Mount of Alchemy, where he patiently mixed the cinnabar of immortality. When he was done, he swallowed forty-nine of the pills. After a purifying bath in the hot springs, a bath lasting seven days and seven nights, he drank a final cup of pure dew and rose to heaven on the back of a dragon.*

We can easily understand how such a tale led the Chinese to endow a thousand sites of the Huang Shan with other myths and legends. (About a hundred of these are collected in a recent volume.) Down through the centuries, they have peopled this honored place with imaginary figures, as well as historical ones. Thus it is said that on Mount Peach Blossom, Sun Wu-k'ung, the famous Monkey King, rested in a grotto behind a waterfall on his journey through the Huang Shan. He took pity on some thirsty climbers and left fruit stolen from the Lady of the West on the top of Mount Miraculous Peaches—and today you will find stones shaped like peaches there. Similarly, the rock Golden-Cockerel-Crowing-at-the-Celestial-Gate bears witness to the tragic separation of two lovers. The Golden Cockerel was once a young man named Ch'uan-ko. His entrancingly beautiful fiancée Yin-mei was wooed and then carried off by a jealous god. The young man pursued them, surmounting every obstacle, until he reached the Celestial Gate, behind which his beloved was captive. Transformed into a cockerel, he sings of his love for eternity. His tears of blood fell upon the ground and turned into the red azaleas that are everywhere in the Huang Shan. Naïve as these tales may seem, we must not laugh at them, knowing they arose from a deeply felt need, knowing also that the Chinese confide to the Huang Shan their most secret sentiments and their hopes for love's fulfillment. Innumerable newlyweds come to this magic mountain after their wedding day. Many heartbroken lovers also come here to take their own lives. Lovers are convinced that in the bosom of this blissful place they will live an immemorial dream. Unhappy lovers believe that to commit suicide here is to ensure a return without regret to life's source.

Thus the Huang Shan, in the heart of China, becomes for the Chinese the miraculous and sacred place where all desire may burgeon, the site itself being the object of desire. Every Chinese who comes to the Huang Shan has a strange feeling of having found his place and himself, of having reached a goal. But if he stays awhile, he is overwhelmed by a passionate love, bewitched by something so real and yet so cruelly unattainable, so full of palpable beauty, so laden with unfathomable mystery, now attracting, then fleeing, now revealing, then hiding.... Small wonder that poets and painters through the ages have compared the mountain to a bewitching woman who haunts the soul and kindles the imagination.

The image of a woman comes to mind when describing the famous Huang Shan tea. It is called Chanühong, the Girl-in-Red-Gathering. Despite its name, this is a green tea whose leaves are tiny when dry. Once steeped, however, the leaves swell in the cup and assume graceful forms which, seen through the dappled steam, look exactly like young girls picking tea in the rosy light of dawn. I first drank this tea one afternoon when, after a long climb, I reached the heights of Luminous Peak. Caught in a violent cloudburst, chilled to the bone, I was given refuge by the people at the weather station there. They offered me tea made with spring water, which gave off a heady fragrance. As we sipped our tea, we admired the fresh sparkle of the landscape after rain. To the south stood the Capital of Heaven and the Lotus Blossom, wreathed in shining clouds. Suddenly someone exclaimed, "Look!" All eyes turned toward the southwest, where the veil of mist was torn from end to end, giving way to a rainbow resting like an archway upon two peaks. Through the arch, we could see in the distance, beyond the fleecy hills grouped like a flock of sheep, beyond the outspread plains, a ribbon of water flowing toward the east. The Changjiang—whose inexorable stream bids us to remember that other side of the mountain, our earthly life, which alone allows us to try to reach out toward the mysteries of heaven. For this, what better guide than the Huang Shan? We remained long silent, profoundly moved by a splendor which we felt should endure forever, but which we knew deep in our hearts to be fleeting.

FRANÇOIS CHENG

THE PHOTOGRAPHER'S NOTEBOOK AND HIS PRAISE OF THE MISTS.
Sun stands on the edge of a precipice. Waves of mist assail him, envelop him as he stands, barely
visible, before a painted backdrop too Chinese to be real. Solemnly, he shouts to me: "Marc, take a
picture of me to put in your tomb!" So here it is, this album, this "tome" as he meant to call it in his
almost perfect French, and Sun, my interpreter and guide in the Huang Shan, a recent graduate of
Beijing University, is indeed in these pages.

Zao Wou-ki convinced me when he said, "You must go to the Huang Shan. It can't be described,
it has to be seen." In 1965, a postage stamp as lovely as an engraving had caught my eye. I showed it
around, asking vainly, "Is it a real mountain? Where is it?" When, in 1983, I finally arrived at the foot
of this range, I discovered that twenty years earlier, a famine resulting in two million deaths had com-
pelled the authorities to close the region to foreign visitors. Today the peasants cultivate their fields. The
result is a surplus of rice. Moreover, there is a surplus of young men, because, I am told, during the famine
some parents allowed the girls to starve, in order to feed the boys. You learn a great deal as you scale the
steps of Mount Huang. It is as if the party line can't stand the altitude. "A political commissar won't
climb," a young Chinese student confides to me. "He stays down below."

Above all, indeed, the Huang Shan means climbing, climbing thousands of steps. The unit of
measure is the step: 4,250 steps up to the North Sea Hotel; 2,230 to the Jade Screen; 2,620 to the Capital
of Heaven; and so on. About 60 miles of trails and stone stairways wind up and down through the range.
Even the shortest segment of path on the flat is paved with flagstone, like a royal way. Here, as at the
Great Wall, we find the same utopian and gratuitous obsession. Although the Great Wall, while visible
from the moon, never stopped the barbarians, the stairs of Mount Huang enable us, barbarians that we
are, conditioned to the concrete of our cities, to reach without feats of alpinism the most dizzying of
heights by mounting steps meticulously adapted to man's stride. At the slightest difficulty, a ramp or a
chain is at hand, or a foothold carved in the rock eases our ascent. This refinement in the art of reducing
physical effort was wrested from the mountain by dint of centuries of titanic labor. Who ordered this
work? Was it an emperor, such as Chin, builder of the Great Wall? "No", an official answers, "the
people of the mountains." A polite silence. All I can learn is that in 1934 the widow of one of Jiang

■

Jieshi's (Chiang Kai-shek's) generals ordered the stairway with chain leading up to the Capital of Heaven to be carved out of the rock. Today, no longer sufficient for the tourist traffic, it is paralleled by a second set of stairs, one-way, for downhill traffic only. Red lights next? In the West, alpinists climb with their eyes riveted to their feet; here the carved steps deliver us from this obsession, allowing us to reach the summit while abandoning ourselves to "the triumph of gratified muscles" and "that exhilarating rapture of the body fulfilled" so beautifully described by Victor Segalen. Our eyes thus liberated, we can feast them on the view before we reach the top. Each step gradually reveals a little more of another world; each step brings new visual fulfillment. For us, the mountain is often a place of challenge, of competition. A new way up, the surmounting of dangers lure us on. The man who conquers a mountain is a superman in our eyes. In contrast, he who climbs to the top of the Huang Shan is only one among thousands gone before him. He comes from afar not for the exploit itself but to follow in the footsteps of the poets and the painters. Time has flowed over these flights of steps, well worn, ageless, which endlessly mount toward promontories raised high, as if in homage to the cult of beauty. Before they reach the Capital of Heaven, the stairs divide into two flights, one of which vanishes into the mist. Does it lead to unfathomable depths or to the heavens? Or do the paths of the world and of dreams part ways here?

Sun, who is luckily more down-to-earth, chooses the right trail. I am his first "long-nose," that being the name by which the guides call their European clientele. He translates the remarks of passers-by with a zeal tempered by candor. A man from Shanghai sharply remarks, "Of course your long-nose can climb faster than we can. While we lived on vegetable bouillon, he ate beef at every meal." Sun tells me that the end of Soviet aid in the early sixties and the slogan "Count on your own strength" produced a famine which affected an entire generation.

In the Huang Shan, during the right season, which is the season of mists, one often runs across a painter sitting, alert and patient, upon a rock by the wayside, a blank sheet of paper before him. One of them ignores us; another shows us his drawings and talks with fervor of his newfound freedom. They are all proud of being able to choose their own subjects once more. Not long ago, as a result of Mao Zedong's famous discourse on art and literature, intellectuals and artists were forced to "serve the people." Subject matter was imposed: workmen, peasants, and soldiers, all with their faces turned to the left. The painter who refused to conform was suspected of rightist deviation. During the Cultural Revolution, painting was forbidden. Only the sycophants of the cult of personality were allowed to paint. Pencils and paintbrushes disappeared, having been hidden or destroyed. Poets and painters were forbidden to come to the Huang Shan. Only the Red Guards scaled the mountain, to carve in rock the sayings of Mao. Thus were the words of the Great Leader to withstand weather and history as long as the granite endured. Ten years later, the words have been obliterated by chisels. "Who did it?" I ask. "The masses." In their haste, the masses forgot the periods and commas, which are now the only traces of Mao's thoughts left on the mountain.

Today many painters and art lovers, students and professors of the Beaux-Arts come here. In China there are more Sunday painters than anywhere else. The number of paintbrushes sold confirms this. A trip to the Huang Shan is an obligatory rite of passage. They come in the footsteps of their masters to rediscover the traditions of the ancients. Here on these heights, the fury of the winds and the mystery of the mists enrapture even the most levelheaded of men. But those with whom I talk do not speak only of painting. They are extremely curious about our world. At a bend in the trail, I am often asked direct questions: "You come, you go, you are free?" "You can say what you want?" "You disagree with your government and you can shout it in the streets?" "For us, spontaneity is out. We must always pretend to think correctly." In the evening in their dormitories, these girls and young men watch televised images from the West: strikers, union rallies, student marches. If the authorities meant to give them a dismal picture of the West and its disorders, these Chinese students have instead had a practical education in the art of protest. Today I think back on my young friends, on their spontaneity, on their irreverence toward governmental authority, and above all on that virus of freedom they caught when they came into contact with us. What has become of them? Aroused by the joy of freedom, did they help build the statue of the Goddess of Democracy, symbol of their shattered dreams? Did they survive the massacrers of Tiananmen Square?

Far from Tiananmen, Sun and I talk about the newfound freedom of painters. He interrupts me: "Marc, for us young people today, even more important than freedom to paint is freedom to love." "Ah, do you mean that now you can make love before marriage?" "No no, we've been given the freedom to talk about love!" And the great laugh which breaks up his face also serves to conceal his modesty. Now I learn of lovers come from afar to scale this mountain, one of the Venices of China. Ahead of us on our path, emerging from the mist, a scarlet blur comes toward us, a couple on their honeymoon. The very beautiful and very blushing bride, who has long braids and carries a pink parasol, allows herself to be photographed after asking her husband's permission. I linger to hear the story of their wedding. "Oh, it was over a year ago, and the next day we went our separate ways, back to our workplaces, over a thousand miles apart. This is the first time we've seen each other since then. We have three days together." I give them a picture of their hero, Zhou Enlai, as a wedding present. Of France, they know only three names: Platini, de Gaulle, and Napoleon.

Not only happy couples, but thwarted lovers, drawn to the precipices, climb the Huang Shan. A statistic: in 1987 there were thirty-six suicides, including several couples. Sun insists that it is not the mist-enshrouded mountain which causes this despair. I ask him, "Why couples?" A passionate love...and then the hostility of parents or the inability to find housing makes marriage impossible. So a tragic vow is made: to see the Huang Shan and die together. In China, suicide has its protocol. For instance, if you slit your veins in front of your enemy's door, you make him responsible for your death and cause him to go to prison. By jumping from the Capital of Heaven, are the unhappy couples taking revenge upon the heavens which they curse? Fortunately, the celestial Capital is the setting for other vows. Hundreds of padlocks are attached to the chain on the guardrail above the precipice. Here and there, a scrap of material is tied to the padlock-red for happiness, white for mourning. These locks symbolize vows of love. I saw a young man, handsome and romantic-looking, coming down alone, clutching in his hand the tiny key of the padlock he had just hung. Lashed by wind and rain, the padlocks, although eaten by rust, still hold fast for years and years. It is pleasant to think that these vows of love have weathered the storms better than the thoughts of Mao.

On the top of Mount Lotus Blossom, a narrow promontory overlooking the entire range from its 6,060 feet, we await the long shadows of falling night. The last hikers are wending their way down. One man stays on. He carries a small black plastic briefcase, wears city shoes and the Beijing functionary's obligatory raincoat and fountain pen. He ignores us, his eyes fixed far, far away on the horizon. Is he *entranced by the beauty of overwhelmed by grief? Sun and I respect his silence and begin our descent. He remains upon the heights, now bathed in fog and darkness. "That guy is weird," Sun says to me. We are worried about him, but from far away we can hear his footsteps against the stones. The next day we learn the story of the man in the raincoat. All that night he wandered, looking for a resting place. A year ago his wife died of cancer, and the day before we saw him, his colleagues at Chemical Factory Number 2 in Beijing told him that his only son had been killed on the Vietnamese border. His coworkers immediately accompanied him, without papers or baggage, to the train leaving for the Huang Shan, as though only the mists of the Lotus Blossom could assuage his grief. Sun tells me that in China tradition has it that a desperate man always offers himself some special treat before he commits suicide. This can be a fabulous meal or a stay in the Huang Shan. Today, as an ultimate refinement, sumptuous feasts are available on the mountain. Chinese porcelain, wine, beer, fish, meat, vegetables, fruit, and sweets are carried on the backs of men and women up more than 4,000 steps from the valley to the West Sea Hotel.*

In the Huang Shan, the bearer, like the poet and the artist, has been ennobled. Along the paths, he is always given the right of way. He alone proudly refuses to have his picture taken. The artful way in which he lashes down and balances the most varied loads is a secret to be envied. He bends and yields to the rhythm of the pliable bamboo. His load often exceeds his own weight. He also carries men. On chairs he carries tired Japanese tourists or overseas Chinese, for whom this mode of transportation is one of the status symbols of newfound wealth. The mountain echoes with the songs of the bearers: "Ah...ih...oh... ah...ih...oh..." or, "Our pal is getting married and tonight we'll drink to him," raucous shouts and rhythmic refrains, a marching chant, the first music *invented by man. The need to sustain effort engendered rhythm and recitative chant. The mountain also rings with the sound of the stonecutters' chisels shattering the granite to reveal its natural rose color. Here the five senses are surfeited. The* scent *of pines, dried leaves, faded flowers, of damp mosses and lichens, and especially of forest fires, whose smoke rises to the clouds. The* touch, *in caressing rocks as smooth and polished as bronze statues; the suppleness of sandal against stone, the coolness of fine rain against the face. The* taste *of tea served at a wayside stop, the flavors of the three hundred medicinal plants which grow on the mountain of painters.*

■

But it is the mist and the clouds which enchant the <u>eye</u>. They purify and delineate the planes of the landscape, expunge the superfluous, erase disorder. By sliding a fleecy veil behind a peak—brilliant brushstroke of Nature!—the mist shows not the chaos of the mountain but only the line of a crest, the volume of a rock, the shape of a pine. A picture is drawn before our eyes. It may be the most beautiful in the world, yet it lasts but a moment. Pushed by a sudden gust of wind, the mist envelops it, and everything disappears. Ephemeral, the scene will never be the same again. In the mountain, the wind is king. It commands the clouds, raises them up, thrusts them aside, summons, then disperses them. The clouds, obedient to the wind, provide all sorts of surprises. We watch for them in the west; they appear in the east. We look for them overhead; they unfurl at our feet. Clouds enjoy slithering up the mountainside. On reaching the saddle, they are suddenly transformed into a vast, billowing expanse, cascading down into the next valley, completely engulfing it. Thus is formed the North Sea, most famous of the cloud seas in the Huang Shan. This sea obeys rules proper to its element: islands, reefs, peninsulas emerge in a tidal rhythm. In the calm of evening, by the water's edge, the poet discovers its shores, its coves. A sudden gust roils its vaporous surface. A crag withstands the waves' assault. Lashed by blue foam, like a ship half seas over, its prow cuts through the ebb and flow. Swamped and drawn under by the mists, the crag disappears, only to reemerge, proud but still buffeted by the swell. Lying on the smooth rock of the West Balcony, I discover in the storm-swept sky other clouds playing a game of mimicry: dragons and horsemen, lianas and sea wrack, scarves and cascading hair mingle, blend, untangle. All is movement, explosion, light; all is gray, blue-gray, white.

When the sun breaks through, we are grateful, for it warms us and dries our clothes. Our bodies welcome the sun, but we swear at it for driving away the mystery, the poetry. Bathed in sunlight, the landscape succumbs to bad taste. Gray and blue nuances are replaced by reds and glaring yellows, much to the delight of postcard fanciers, whose great reward is the sunset. To see the sun rise over the sea of clouds between Sublime Peak and Mount Now-I-Believe-It crowns our visit with a note, not of bad taste but of grandiloquence: a rite resembling a majestic overture to dawn, accompanied by thunderous organ music—and by choirs, for a rising clamor echoes through the mountains, keeping time with the sun's first rays. These are the joyous cries of the Chinese tourists who braved the cold night, wrapped in

■

their red-and-blue quilts, to hail from the heights of the North Sea this privileged moment. The privilege is real, for more often than not, the fog forms an impenetrable barrier, and they wait in vain.

When the clouds disperse, the sun reveals the extensive damages wrought by pollution. In Chinese cities, these are signs of modernity, hence a source of pride. The thousands of tourists who flock to the Huang Shan leave behind them in the ravines and at the feet of the ancient pines the appurtenances of urban "civilization": bottles, cans, bits of plastic of all colors. Without knowing it, they are desecrating the object of their reverence. Luckily the mists, without which the mountain would simply exist as it is, often cover the valleys and hide the blemishes with a modest veil.

Why does this mountain, more than any other, attract so many men and women of all ages and from every province? Chinese man, who in the city and even in the country gives in to the pressure of the anonymous masses, finds in himself, when he stands before these mists and peaks, a new individuality. Here, as nowhere else in China, I have met individuals, not a collectivity. If down through the ages this place has inspired pictorial and poetic creativity, it is not only because the mist refines and shapes the splendors of the landscape, but also because the man who allows himself to be enveloped and captivated by the mist is plunged into a harmony and mystery that the painter-poet Wang Wei of the Tang dynasty called "interior resonance." Standing atop the Capital of Heaven, lashed by the wind, face-to-face with the most beautiful landscape in the world, who has not experienced this strange resonance and the irrepressible urge to intone a song in praise of the mists?

MARC RIBOUD

Lovers of Chinese paintings know that the Huang Shan is very distant and very different from the sugar loaves of Guilin, but Western tourists are often unaware of this. Hangzhou, a forty-five-minute flight from Shanghai, is the preferred departure point for an excursion to the Huang Shan. From there a six-hour taxi ride or a ten-hour drive on the bus brings you to the foot of the mountain. The road (170 miles) is good, and very beautiful toward the end of the trip, when it goes through Ming towns and villages unchanged since the fourteenth century. A stop at Shexian is recommended. Decent hotel accommodations for the night are available in the area called Hot Springs, at an altitude of 2,060 feet. The next morning, a drive of 5 miles takes you to the cable car built by the Japanese in 1987 (3,170 feet). The cable car climbs to an altitude of 5,940 feet in twelve minutes. From there a half-hour walk will bring you to the North Sea (Bei Hai) Hotel and, a bit farther on, to the West Sea (Xi Hai) Hotel (picture on page opposite), built in 1989 by a Swedish firm and managed by a Hong Kong company. Until 1988, accommodations in the Huang Shan were Spartan: unheated dormitories or rooms, often without water. Today the West Sea Hotel, with its 170 modern and heated rooms, its running water guaranteed in all seasons (thanks to a dam), its choice of Bordeaux wines, and its hostesses (young mountain girls dressed up as turn-of-the-century Chinese courtesans), is an unexpected surprise when the weary hiker comes upon it at a bend in the trail. From here the famous pathways and stone stairs radiate out toward the various peaks, passes, and promontories, all of which can be reached in a walk of one to four hours. Guides and bearers are always available. When returning to the valley, a small detour to the Jade Screen Hotel (rudimentary comfort) allows the more energetic tourist to climb the Lotus Blossom (6,060 feet) and the Capital of Heaven (5,990 feet), the two highest and most beautiful peaks of the range.

The tourist should take a good solid pair of sneakers, an umbrella, a light raincoat, and a supply of Granola bars.

The mist is at its best in autumn. Spring is also a good season. Frost begins in November, and there can be snow in March.

By 1990, direct flights from Beijing, Shanghai, and Hong Kong to the town of Tun Xi (50 miles from the Huang Shan) will be available. It will be possible to leave Hong Kong in the morning and reach the West Sea Hotel by evening.

■

PRINTED BY JEAN GENOUD SA, LAUSANNE, SWITZERLAND